Pioneer Plowmaker

Pioneer Plowmaker

A Story about John Deere

by David R. Collins
illustrations by Steve Michaels

A Carolrhoda Creative Minds Book

Carolrhoda Books, Inc./Minneapolis

*To the farmers of the world and the members of
John Deere's working family who continue the
legacy left by a gentleman blacksmith*

Carolrhoda Books, Inc. c/o The Lerner Group
241 First Avenue North, Minneapolis, MN 55401

Library of Congress Cataloging-in-Publication Data

Collins, David R.
    Pioneer plowmaker: a story about John Deere/ by David R.
Collins
        p.   cm. — (A Carolrhoda creative minds book)
    Includes bibliographical references.
    Summary: A biography of the inventor and manufacturer who
produced one of the first self-scouring plows.
    ISBN 0-87614-424-5
    1. Deere & Company—History—Juvenile literature. 2.
Deere, John, 1804-1886. 3. Industrialists—United States—
Biography—Juvenile literature. 4. Agricultural machinery
industry—United States—History—Juvenile literature. [1.
Deere, John, 1804-1886. 2. Industrialists. 3. Inventors. 4.
Agricultural machinery industry—History.] I. Title. II.
Series.
HD9486.U6D43   1990
[92]—dc20   90-32501
                                               CIP
                                               AC

Manufactured in the United States of America

3 4 5 6 7 8 9 10 – P/MA – 01 00 99 98 97 96 95 94

Table of Contents

6

① Mystery in Middlebury

Air rushed into the stone hearth as the blacksmith pulled on the bellows handle. Flames shot up, sending sparks into the air. The huge smith, with soot covering his hands and sweaty forehead, pushed his long, black tongs into the fire. At the end of them, an iron hoe blade soon glowed red. Then with one smooth movement, the blacksmith yanked the blade out of the flames and laid it on his anvil.

Up went his thick, muscular arm with hammer in hand. Down the hammer came, smashing against the iron blade and throwing sparks in all directions. Up and down, up and down, up and down the hammer went, until finally the iron blade lay straight and fine.

From his place in the shop's doorway, John Deere watched as the blacksmith mended the broken hoe. It fascinated him to see the heated metal change form.

Captain Lawrence paid little attention to the seven-year-old boy observing him. Children often stopped by his smithy to stare as he and his apprentices put iron shoes on horses, built chains, or mended pots and pans.

But this little towheaded boy had returned more than once to Captain Lawrence's forge. John wanted to be a blacksmith someday, and he often came home late from school smelling of fire and heated iron.

John couldn't stay long at his afternoon visits to the blacksmith's forge however. His mother needed him at home. The year was 1811, and times were hard. For three years, his mother, Sarah Deere, had sewed and mended other people's clothes to keep her family together.

The Deere family lived in the small Vermont town of Middlebury. The town was nestled in the peaceful hills of New England. To the east, the Green Mountains stood like watchful guards. To the distant northwest lay the shimmering blue water of Lake Champlain.

More than three years ago, John's father, William Deere, Sr., had been a respected tailor in Middle-bury. William and Sarah had operated a tailoring shop out of the front of their home.

In these early years of 1800, money was scarce in Vermont. Eight out of ten men farmed, trying to scrape out a living on a rocky piece of ground, with a plow and a few animals—usually sheep.

When local harvests were good, the farmers ordered clothes, and the Deere family worked busily. But when harvests failed, the farm families made do with the things they had. They often paid their bills with buckets of milk or bags of grain. Because of this, the Deeres, like many others in Vermont, had fallen into debt.

When news reached William, Sr., that a British relative had died and left him a small inheritance, William made plans to return to his former country. He wanted to use the extra money to get out of debt.

As he sat on a Boston dock, waiting to board the ship for England, William, Sr., wrote a letter home. It was dated June 16, 1808. He addressed the letter to William Deere, Jr., his namesake and eldest son, and wrote about his hopes of "making our family Comfortable." He advised his son, "Let Truth and Honesty be your guide & on no pretense Deviate from it...." Slipping a few dollars inside, William posted the letter and went aboard.

When William Deere, Sr., had not returned home by the autumn of 1808, talk about the tailor began to make its way among the 1,300 residents of Middlebury. Over fenceposts, dinner tables, and store counters, tongues wagged. What had happened to William Deere?

The answer remains a mystery. He sailed away to England and never returned. It was thought that he had arrived safely in England, but no one is sure what happened next. Perhaps the return ship was sunk or captured. England and France were at war, so any voyage across the Atlantic was risky. Or maybe the gentle tailor died at sea. The ship's crew, fearing an unknown disease, could easily have thrown his body into the waves. Such things were known to happen.

Born February 7, 1804, John was only four years

old at the time of his father's disappearance. For the rest of his life, he would carry just a slip of a memory of his father, picturing a tall man with curly hair.

When it became clear that William Deere, Sr., was not coming back, relatives talked about sending the five Deere children off to live with various family members and friends. Sarah would hear none of this. Was she not able to stitch a seam as straight as her husband could? She thought so! And her oldest children could help with the bills. William, Jr., was already twelve years old and apprenticed to Master Warren, the cabinetmaker. Francis, at eight, often worked for the local sugar merchant, helping with the making of maple sugar and tending the trees. So Sarah was able to keep the family together.

As the years passed, the younger children grew to help their mother more and more. Betsy learned to sew seams as fine as her mother's, and the two younger boys, John and George, delivered many a package to Sarah's customers in Middlebury.

It was on his way home from these deliveries that John usually took a detour to Captain Lawrence's smithy. Things were always going on there — whether it was a group of men talking about the country's troubles with England or a stagecoach driver describing his exciting journey through the mountains. John would listen to it all as he watched the blacksmith at work.

In 1812 the United States went to war against England. Business improved at the blacksmith's shop, with more horses to be shod and bayonets to be sharpened. At Deere's tailoring shop, customers were fewer. William, Jr., and Francis had found work where they could earn a room and meals as well as their wages. That left only four mouths to feed in the Deere household.

In 1815 John decided it was time he looked for a regular job to do after school. John's first choice was to work for Captain Lawrence, but he was too young to be a blacksmith's apprentice.

A Middlebury tanner named Epaphras Miller, however, needed someone to grind bark and oak leaves. The powder that was left after the grinding contained a substance called tannin. The tannin helped preserve animal hides and make them soft and supple. It also gave the leather a rich color.

Grown men often tired while turning the grinding wheel at the tannery. Could a boy of eleven do such a job? Master Miller was unsure, but John wanted to try.

Within weeks John proved that he had the stamina and the muscles needed to keep grinding for long periods at a time. Most of the money John earned went into the household fund. But he saved a bit as well. That Christmas John surprised everyone in his family with special presents bought at Hager's Mercantile. And he, himself, paraded about in new shoes and a handsome new suit.

Sarah Deere had reason to be proud of John. But if she entertained thoughts of John graduating from Middlebury Academy someday, she was in for another surprise. John had other plans. He would finish his training in the local grammar school. But that was it.

John's head was ringing with the sounds of sizzling fires and clanging iron. He wanted to see what *his* hands could do in a smithy's stable. "John Deere, Smithy." Yes, those words had a nice ring to them, like the solid clang of a hammer against a steel-topped anvil.

② Learning the Trade

As the older Deere children moved into the adult world, Sarah decided to make a move herself. In May of 1816, a notice appeared in Middlebury's *National Standard,* describing Sarah's decision to move her family and business to a new rental property:

> Mrs. Deere has removed to the house of Mr. S. Hopkins opposite Mr. Schuyler's house where she will be happy to serve her old customers and the public in various branches of the tailoring business on short notice.

16

Although still in Middlebury, the new Deere home stood closer to Otter Creek, where John swam in the summer and skated in the winter. Even better, John now lived closer to Captain Benjamin Lawrence's smithy. He could easily stop by after school or work.

One day in 1821, John came home, his blue eyes blazing and his blond hair tangled with sweat. He had not even taken the time to scrub the dirt and grime of the forge off his hands and arms. The news burst from him—Captain Lawrence wanted John to become one of his apprentice blacksmiths!

At seventeen John had been offered a three-year contract to work daily at the forge. The wage added up to thirty dollars the first year, with a raise of five dollars in each year following. As to a room and meals, John would live with the Lawrence family in their home, on the hill above the blacksmith's shop—as all the captain's apprentices did. He would also get clothing in the agreement, along with some instruction in reading, writing, and arithmetic.

The contract sounded fair, and the captain was a man to respect. So after a family discussion, John accepted the blacksmith's offer and moved to the Lawrence home to start learning his trade.

John took quickly to his new job. At first he did only simple tasks, straightening a skillet handle or shaping an ax head. But soon the apprentice tried his hand at sharpening hayforks and rakes. Then came the more complicated jobs of forming shoes and fitting them onto the horses and oxen. A jittery horse or an obstinate ox could test a blacksmith's skill and patience. Finally, John mastered the art of fixing the ironwork for the stagecoaches, a job that always needed to be done in a hurry. No coach driver wanted to stay long in Middlebury waiting for a new wheel rim or hitching gear.

Throughout his training, John learned the meaning of the saying, "Strike while the iron is hot." It was always easier to start and finish a job on the first heating than to reheat and try again.

Every morning before daybreak, John walked down from the house to the forge. In the dark and quiet shop, he carefully arranged the coals in the forge fireplace, one upon another. Without a hot, hearty fire, little work could be done. Yet there was an art to the chore. Captain Lawrence had showed him how to start and tend the proper-size fire—not too big and not too small. A giant blaze burned up too much coal and threw too many sparks. A few smoldering coals could not mold even a baby's spoon. Once his fire burned strongly, John set to his day's work. It would be a while till the others joined him.

Most nights John Deere was the last to leave the forge, painstakingly checking that no embers remained in the hearth. Too many careless blacksmiths had lost their shops to hidden coals and unexpected sparks.

When John arrived at the Lawrence home, a hot meal was usually waiting. Rumors had it that Melissa Lawrence, the blacksmith's daughter, took more than the usual care in making John comfortable. But little came of her attention. John's thoughts were directed toward one goal—becoming a blacksmith.

By his second year as an apprentice, people began to note that John had a creative style all his own. Farmers remarked that the old tools they brought for repair left the hands of John Deere in better shape than when they were new.

Captain Lawrence bought refined iron by the pound, paying premium prices. John quickly turned the iron into handsome pots and pans. Not even the small leftover bits of iron went to waste. John showed that these bits could be turned into other things—nails, for instance.

As much as John enjoyed working at the forge, it troubled him that many of the wagons he worked on were leaving Middlebury. People were heading west, hoping to find new lands and a better life. Stories of wide-open plains with rich soil were luring people out of New England.

In 1822 a fever spread throughout Middlebury, with illness touching almost every family. John's brother Francis was one of those who died. John returned home for several weeks to help his mother and Betsy with the tailoring.

As for William, Jr., he had become a teacher. In 1823 he opened two schools in Middlebury. One was suited "for the exclusive accommodation of young ladies," while young gentlemen could "receive proper attention" across the street.

"I should perhaps enroll myself," John told a friend. It was just a fleeting thought, however, for he enjoyed his work too much at the captain's forge.

By 1825, twenty-one-year-old John had completed his apprenticeship and did not lack for job offers. He had earned a fine reputation while working for Captain Lawrence. But John had chosen a difficult profession. Before he could become a blacksmith on his own, John had to work as a journeyman—a skilled laborer—for another blacksmith.

When two Middlebury blacksmiths offered John work, he could not make up his mind. David Wells and Ira Allen were both respected smiths. In fact their homes and shops stood side by side on Court Street. Wells's smithy was known for its ironwork for stages, and Allen's was known for its carriage-making. John figured that he could get the most experience by working for both blacksmiths, taking on the most demanding jobs. It was an unusual arrangement, but neither smith complained. They were glad to have John Deere anytime. People would come from miles around to ask for his services.

During this time, a young woman named Demarius Lamb entered John's life. She had come to Middlebury to go to school and now lived with her older brother. The rest of her family lived in Granville, a town in the Green Mountains.

A year younger than John, Demarius stood a foot shorter as well, with long dark hair and brown eyes. Her witty remarks and lively ways attracted the young journeyman. Only she could coax him out of the forge for a picnic or carriage ride. Though John's notes to her were sprinkled with misspelled words and poor grammar, Demarius seemed not to notice.

In 1826 John's mother died. It was a difficult time for John, and Demarius helped him through it.

In the past, John had given most of his wages to his mother. Now she was gone, and his brothers and sister were in positions to take care of themselves. John felt free to think about his future. But the fifteen dollars per month he was earning would hardly support a new wife. And John was determined to marry Demarius.

One morning later that year, Colonel Ozias Buel rode up to the Allen blacksmith shop in Middlebury. Buel had recently purchased thirty acres of land near the village of Burlington, along Lake Champlain. He planned to build a sawmill and a linseed-oil mill on his new property. All he needed was someone to do the ironwork for the two mills.

His search was over. As he watched John Deere work, Colonel Buel knew he had found the blacksmith he wanted.

3

Debts and Disasters

Clang! Clang! Clang! That was the sound John heard for the next year—the hammer pounding iron against the anvil, day after day. A full-fledged blacksmith at twenty-two, John took the title seriously. He was on his own. Every bolt, every hinge, every side rail put into the mills went through the hands of John Deere. His forge fire at Burlington was sparked before daybreak every morning. It burned all day and into the evening. Not a minute was wasted.

Yet there were times when John looked out over the water of Lake Champlain and watched the black smoke of the steamboats snake northward. The young blacksmith wondered about the lands to the west. What would it be like to pull up roots and travel? In Middlebury he had watched the wagons rolling across dusty roads toward the western frontier. Now in Burlington, he stared at steamboats gliding north to meet western waterways. Perhaps a better life could be found somewhere else.

But as quickly as daydreams came to John, they were burned away in the heat of the forge. Clang! Clang! Clang!

Completing the setup of the mills, John headed back to Middlebury. He could marry Demarius now, and he did. On January 28, 1827, the two were wed.

The new couple could afford to furnish a cabin for themselves, but there were no extra funds for a blacksmith's shop. So John accepted a job working for John McVene, a smith in nearby Vergennes.

Unfortunately, respected though John McVene was, his business floundered. Poor harvests gave farmers little money to spend. They often did their own smithing if they could. Those farmers who came to McVene's smithy often bartered for goods and services. Many times the smiths were paid in chickens, grain, or vegetables.

When John and Demarius were expecting their first child, John left his job at Vergennes. He would need guaranteed money to support a wife and child. So John moved the family to Salisbury, Vermont. There the Briggs Shovel Factory was hiring, and John was put to work making tools.

Late in February 1828, Demarius gave birth to their first child—Francis Albert. He was named after John's late brother.

In no time at all, John tired of the factory. The pay was steady, but he had no chance to put a personal mark of quality on the tools he made or experiment with a tool's design to get a better product. John wanted his own shop.

When he heard of a piece of land available at Four Corners in nearby Leicester, John went to investigate. The spot was perfect. Rich farms surrounded the area. Not only that, but the land sat at the crossroads of the main stagecoach lines, which traveled through Vergennes, Middlebury, and Leicester on the way to larger cities in New Hampshire and Massachusetts. John knew that when he wasn't working for the farmers, there would be wagons and carriages to repair. Demarius agreed to move again.

But money posed a problem. Although John had managed to support his growing family, he hadn't been able to put away much extra money. So he borrowed money from a man named Jay Wright, who was willing to become a kind of silent partner. With this loan, John purchased the land and began building his shop.

During the summer and autumn of 1829, John built a steady business in Leicester, in addition to a cabin for his family. His neighbors pitched in to help him get established. A good blacksmith was a treasure in any community.

One winter night, John awoke with a start. Someone was pounding on the cabin door.

"It's your smithy!" the man outside shouted. "It's on fire!"

John rushed to the window to see the roaring blaze of red against the black night. Stuffing his nightshirt into a pair of trousers, John sprinted the short distance to the forge. He stood barefoot in the snow in front of the smithy he had worked so hard to build. How could it have happened? He had always made sure the forge fire was out before he went home. For a long time, he stood staring at the fire as it swallowed up his business.

Early the next morning, John returned to the site, weary from lack of sleep. He wanted to salvage anything he could. Some small coals still glowed in spots, but the winter winds had cooled the remaining ruins. Neighbors joined John. Farmers brought what wood they could spare. Coach drivers and merchants offered their time to help him rebuild his shop. Jay Wright came to the rescue again.

In a few weeks, John was back at work in his own blacksmith's shop.

Not long after John's smithy was rebuilt, the squeals of a new baby filled the Deere cabin. John and Demarius named their second child Jennette.

Jennette was only a few months old when disaster struck the family again. As thunder roared above the Vermont countryside, rain pelted Leicester's wooden roofs. Lightning ripped into the Deere smithy, and it burst into flames. John walked among ashes once more.

He rebuilt his smithy again. But he was too far in debt to pull himself out. His customers did not pay him in the hard cash he needed. John had hardly paid Jay Wright back for the last loan, and he was forced to ask for another. This time, Jay Wright lent him $78.76, enough to tide the Deere family over until John could find work with steady pay.

Amos Bosworth gave John his next opportunity. Coming into town in 1831 by way of the stage, Amos learned of the young blacksmith's misfortune from the coach driver. Amos walked on over to John's smithy at Four Corners to talk a little business. Bosworth owned a hotel and several other properties in the town of Royalton, to the east. He also had shares in the town's stagecoach lines.

Now if John were willing to keep the coaches and carriages repaired, Bosworth would pay John steady wages and let his family live in one of the houses Bosworth owned.

The offer sounded good to John.

Within a week, the Deere family piled into a wagon with John at the reins. Over the Green Mountains they traveled, through the Brandon Gap and into the White River Valley. Within another week, they settled into their home in Royalton, and John Deere stood at the anvil, pounding iron. As part of the Cascadnac House Hotel, the smithy became a business center for travelers as well for local citizens.

In 1832 Demarius and John were expecting again. Ellen Sarah, a second daughter, was born.

John had little time to rest. The more he worked, the farther John's reputation traveled. Word moved swiftly "that this man Deere works magic with a hammer."

But a good reputation wasn't enough for John. He still wanted his own shop. As he worked, John was reminded again and again of the western frontier. Wagons came in needing repair or spare parts for the long trek west. Stagecoaches required ironwork before they could set out on the same journey. Perhaps John would go west someday. But right now, he had debts to pay and three children to support.

After two years of working for Bosworth, John heard about a piece of land near a mountain stream in the village of Hancock. Since there were no other forges in the area, it seemed a safe bet for a strong smithing business. And with water close by, John hoped to avoid another tragedy by fire.

So John used what little money he had to buy the property and build his smithy. Just down the road, a large house stood empty and ready for renters. The Deere family moved in, and shortly afterward, another daughter was born. They named her Frances Alma.

Up at sunrise and working long after sunset, John often forgot to stop for meals. As each machine part or tool came into John's shop, he studied it closely. He could quickly distinguish what was good and bad about each one. The cheap and shoddy tools made by factories angered him. Little care had been taken to make strong handles or sturdy iron fittings. Why make something if it's going to break? John wondered. He worked long and hard to make sure that his tools and fittings were built to last.

Farmers bragged about John Deere's workmanship. John had constructed a dam across the stream near his smithy and attached a water wheel. As the water rushed over the dam and turned the wheel, his grindstone whirled. He could polish steel tools to a fine edge without wearing out his arms. Farmers boasted that John polished the prongs of their pitchforks "until they slipped in and out of the hay like needles." Deere's shovels and hoes, folks said, were "like no others that could be bought—they scoured themselves of the soil by reason of their smooth, satiny surfaces."

But a fine reputation does not pay off loans. Kind words do not buy bars of iron or coal for a forge. In truth, John worked too much at the forge and too little at collecting debts—or paying off his own. John had to sell the land back to the man from whom he had bought it and start paying rent.

By October 1836, John's silent partner from Leicester had become far from silent about the money John still owed him. Jay Wright went to court to sue John for his money. Either John would pay him by November 7 or the court action would put the blacksmith in jail.

John didn't know what to do. He couldn't work any harder. And he couldn't collect unpaid debts from customers who didn't have any money.

One day, as the November deadline grew near, Amos Bosworth stopped by John's shop. John's former employer mentioned that he was heading west to a place called Grand Detour in Illinois. Another Vermonter, Leonard Andrus, had founded this settlement at a bend in the Rock River. Andrus was now building a sawmill. The village had plenty of waterpower, Amos explained, but it had no blacksmith to do the ironwork for the mill. New settlers were arriving all the time, he added, and they needed tools for farming. The soil was said to be rich and fertile.

The West looked tempting to John. He considered his chances of making a living in Vermont. They didn't look good. No matter how hard he worked, his debts increased. Jay Wright and others wanted their money—now! Maybe a better future waited for him elsewhere.

Yet John couldn't just move the whole Deere family to a place he'd never been before, especially not now. Demarius was expecting their fifth child. Perhaps John could go on his own. He could see what it was like and then either send for the family or return.

John made his decision. Without delay he sold

his smithing business to his father-in-law for two hundred dollars. He gave part of the money to Demarius to take care of the family, and the rest he put in his pocket for the trip. Then he packed up his tools.

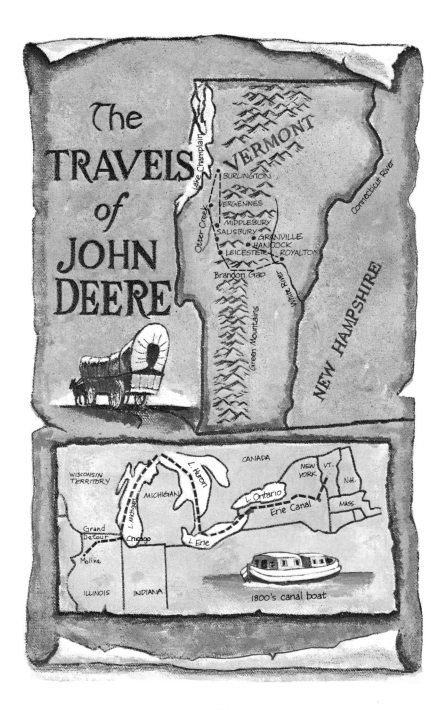

④

Into the Soil

John Deere traveled light as he headed west. The thirty-two-year-old blacksmith from Vermont joined hordes of American pioneers trekking westward, armed mostly with determination and hope. By stagecoach, canal boat, and river steamer, John traveled cross-country to the Erie Canal; through Lakes Erie, Huron, and Michigan; and south to the swampy village of Chicago. The rest of the journey was by wagon, rolling in and out of tired ruts worn by the United States Army during the Blackhawk War.

News of the blacksmith's arrival in Grand Detour spread quickly among the thirty-five cabins dotting the Rock River shores. The news caused quite a stir since the nearest smithy was a forty-mile journey over rough terrain. No sooner had John set down his pack than his friend Amos was telling him of a job that needed doing. The lower shaft of Leonard Andrus's sawmill was broken.

Until repaired, the mill would sit idle.

John wasted no time. Since he had no forge, one had to be built. John picked up stones from along the river and cemented them together. In less than two days, he had fixed the shaft, and the sawmill began ripping out boards for new homes. Like a squirrel leaping from branch to branch, the word spread—a master mechanic had come to Grand Detour.

Farmers swarmed to the blacksmith's forge. John scarcely had time to put up a roof to keep the rain from his fire. Each day brought a new collection of broken and twisted tools; pots and pans that needed new handles; horses and oxen for shoeing.

Can you make me an iron ring? someone would ask. I need some chains welded, said another. Work, work, work. When he finally got some time, John built an 18-by-24-foot frame house, with a fireplace in the living room and steep stairs leading to two bedrooms. John longed for the day when he could afford to send for his family.

During the winter of 1836, heavy snows brought life in Grand Detour to a slow crawl. But the forge fires blazed on, and John Deere's hammer kept clanging.

At the first scent of spring, farmers brought in

their plows for sharpening or for iron stripping. Yet John was surprised by the downcast mood of his customers. Back East, farmers had always looked forward to another planting season, even though the soil was rocky and thin. John had seen the rich, black soil around Grand Detour. What could be wrong?

Sure, it's good soil, one farmer declared. But I'd rather plow back East where all you have to do is get through a few rocks and stones. Why, here the soil sticks to the plow blade like glue.

You can't plow but a few yards before you have to stop and scrape the dirt off, another barked. It doesn't matter if you use horses or oxen, two teams or ten, it's still the same.

Every farmer had the same complaint. The soil held together like thick clumps of clay, sticking to every plow. The farmers had the best farmland in the country, maybe in the whole world, but they were nearly ready to sell it and move on. If only there were a plow that could cut into the earth and scour itself clean.

Amos Bosworth shook his head. He didn't think it could be done. Neither did Lewis Crandall, a farmer whose field was across from John's shop. No one thought it was possible.

John had heard the word impossible before. Sometimes farmers would tell him certain tools were impossible to fix. But John would fix them. Another time an iron wagon-wheel rim would be impossible to bend back into shape. But John would manage to do it. A challenge spurred the blacksmith on—to prove he could do the impossible.

Each day, as John tended the fire, sharpened shovels, or pounded out the curves in bent handles, he thought about the farmers and their problem—that thick, rich, sticky soil. Cast-iron plows worked well enough in the sandy soils of the East, but the blades swiftly developed pits or holes. And cast iron could not be shined or smoothed so that heavy soil would slip off of it. A steel blade could be polished and sharpened, but John had not been impressed with the steel plow blades he had seen. Clearly the blades had not satisfied the farmers either. Such thoughts were on John's mind one April morning in 1837 when he went to see Leonard Andrus at his sawmill.

After completing his business with Andrus, John turned to leave. A flash of light caught his eye. Sunlight splashing into the mill was reflecting off a large circular-saw blade. The broken blade, made of Sheffield steel, sat resting in an empty corner.

Steel was hard to come by, since it was generally shipped from England. But even if there had been steel around to experiment with, John could not have afforded to buy it. This discarded saw blade could give him the metal he needed.

Andrus gladly gave John the useless blade. In the days that followed, there was no shoeing of horses or repairing of tools. John Deere put all his energy into designing and making a new plow.

First the blacksmith cut the teeth off the saw blade with a hand chisel, making the circular blade into a slanted rectangle. Laying the steel section on the fire, he heated the metal until it blazed red. Then he pounded it into a curved plow blade that could cut into the soil and throw the dirt to the side.

Digging up a sapling, John whittled the roots into two handles. At the base of the handles, John attached the new steel plow blade. Then he supported the blade with another piece of wood and added a wooden beam that could be hooked up to the horses and oxen. He connected the beam to the blade with a metal pole. To make the plow even sturdier, John cut holes in the shaft and the beam, and inserted wooden plugs to hold the individual parts together.

For hours John polished the edges of the steel blade. How the metal shone! Surely no soil could stick to its shiny sides. The dirt would have to slide right off.

Finally John Deere sat back to look at his work. He had put together a very rough plow. He took it to Lewis Crandall's field and tested it in the thick, moist soil. Instead of using the usual team of horses or oxen to pull the plow, John plowed a long, straight row with just one horse. It worked! Not once did he get stuck or have to scrape dirt off the blade. But John thought the plow could still be improved. He brought it back to the shop to work on it some more.

Slowly, carefully, with an eye to every detail, John perfected the design for the new plow. Again and again, he stopped to polish, to pull, to pound, and to shape. The tilt of the handles had to be just right, and so did the length of the shaft and the sharpness of the blade.

At last the plow was ready. He leaned it against a box by the side of his shop door.

A few days later, an old farmer drove up. "Who made that plow?" he asked.

"I did, such as it is," John answered. "Wood-work and all."

The farmer picked up the plow, amazed at its glistening blade and how little it weighed. "Well," said the farmer, "that looks as though it'd work. Let me take it home and try it, and if it works all right, I'll keep it and pay you for it. If not, I'll return it."

"Take it," John said confidently, "and give it a thorough trial."

Two weeks later, the man returned, without the plow. He paid the blacksmith. "Now," the farmer ordered, "get a move on you and make more plows just like the last one."

It was a moment John Deere would never forget and a story he would tell for years. He had created a tool that could carve into the soil and scour itself clean, throwing off dirt as it cut through the fields. Many had tried to make a steel plow like this before, and a few had succeeded. But no plow would last longer or be better remembered.

⑤

Building the Best

By the summer of 1838, John felt he was in Grand Detour to stay. Farmers came regularly to his forge, and in his spare time, he worked on making plows. His business prospered.

Yet the blacksmith missed his family. "Come ahead," he wrote to Demarius. "All is ready here."

Come they did, on a journey that took six weeks. When he heard that his family had arrived in nearby Dixon, John galloped off to meet them. He rushed to embrace his wife and children. A tired Demarius handed her husband a bundle in a blanket. It was Charles Henry, the son John had not yet seen.

"Here, John," she said, "*you* hold him a while. I've carried him all the way from Vermont."

Once his family had settled in, John set about his daily smithing. With every spare moment, he worked on improving the steel plow he had made. He built an addition to the back of his smithy, where he could house a horse on a treadmill. He used this horsepower to turn his grinding stone so he could polish his plows to their sharpest and shiniest.

Lightweight and slick, John Deere's plow became known as the "singing plow" for the high-pitched whine it made as it moved swiftly through the soil. John hired assistants. Each year he made a greater number of plows, putting more and more time into this new work. By 1842 he was selling one hundred a year.

John was not alone in developing new plows. The Jewett & Hitchcock Company soon designed a plow with interchangeable parts. With the Jewett plow, the tool would not have to be discarded when one part broke. The failed part was merely replaced. Quick to grasp a business opportunity, John began selling the Jewett plow as well as his own. He also began using a system of interchangeable parts on his plows.

Although bigger and better-known brands of plows were being made in the factories back East, no plow was built to last longer than John Deere's. John took no shortcuts at his forge. He also took the time to talk with the farmers who came to his shop. They knew what they needed to do their work better and more easily. John listened closely to the farmers and used their ideas.

By 1843, at the age of thirty-nine, John Deere was no longer a mere blacksmith. He had become a businessman in a larger sense—the founder of a plow company. Legal papers were signed and copyrights obtained. Leonard Andrus became his partner, and the two men built a two-story plow factory about a block from John's smithy. Soon the factory had about ten employees and was equipped with both steam engines and horsepower. In that first year, the two partners manufactured four hundred plows and sold them for around ten dollars each.

Though John now had a factory and employees to make his plows, he still made sure every plow was built to last.

The brother of John's bookkeeper said, "He kept everybody who worked for him busy. No lazy man need apply for a job with John."

As the demand for plows increased, so did the need for steel to make the plows. Getting steel on the frontier was a major difficulty. At first John had used whatever he could find. But with the start-up of his factory, he made arrangements for steel to be delivered to him. It had to be shipped across the Atlantic Ocean from England by steamship; up the Mississippi and Illinois rivers by packet boats; and over the final forty miles to Grand Detour by wagon. The steel cost John almost three hundred dollars a ton. It was a daring undertaking, especially for one who did not always handle business affairs well. But by importing the steel, John could increase the number of plows he could make and sell.

Many blacksmiths of the time took orders for plows and then built them. But from his first plow, John Deere introduced a new idea. He made plows without orders and then sold them. He and Andrus often took the famous "self-polisher" plow out into the country themselves to sell it to the farmers in the area.

Whether doing his blacksmithing, overseeing his employees, or selling his plows, John worked long, hard days. He often started at four in the morning and did not stop until ten in the evening.

When he was not in his leather apron and bent over the forge, John dressed with an eye for finery. His solid, six-foot frame had grown stockier over the years, due to his love of hearty meals.

In 1843, the year filled with so many changes, another important event happened. Jay Wright, John's former partner from Vermont, caught up with him. Wright took John to court for the $78.76 John had borrowed and never repaid. Now the bill was over $1,000 because of the interest and penalties added. But this time, John had the money to pay. The twelve-year-old debt was finally put to rest.

Jay Wright was not the only person who went to court to get people to pay their debts. John also spent his share of time suing to be paid. Since the fees for shoeing a horse or fixing a chain were usually small, blacksmithing was often done on credit. Unfortunately, though, many times these small sums were conveniently forgotten by those who owed them. Collecting bills proved to be a challenge for John Deere most of his life.

By the mid-1840s, the Deere partnership had expanded, and it was clear that Grand Detour was not the best place to continue manufacturing plows. It was too far from supplies and transportation.

Wagons hauling materials often got stuck in muddy roads. Most seasons of the year, the Rock River was not deep enough for steamboats, and proposed railroad routes weren't going to come near Grand Detour.

John began to consider whether to stay in Grand Detour or move to Moline, Illinois. Only seventy miles from Grand Detour, Moline would offer the company better transportation routes, since the town was along the Mississippi River.

The Deere family was ready for a move as well. The Deeres had outgrown their home in Grand Detour. The nursery had become crowded. Emma had been born in 1840; Hiram had followed her in 1842 (and had died in 1844); and Alice had arrived in 1844.

By 1846 John welcomed his eldest son, Francis Albert, into the business. Albert, as he was known, had graduated from Rock Island Seminary, and at eighteen, he took over the company's bookkeeping chores. This was a relief for John. He had never handled money well, and he had always had difficulties leaving financial decisions to his partners.

But on January 13, 1848, tragedy struck. After a short, unexpected illness, Albert died. It was a severe blow for John.

Albert's death seemed to settle the matter of moving. John left his old factory and partnership behind with Leonard Andrus, preferring to start fresh in Moline. By spring John had established another partnership and started building a new factory on the shores of the Mississippi. Although the factory began making its first plows the summer of 1848, John later advertised the founding of the Moline Plow Works as 1847. He never explained why.

In the summer of 1848, the Deere family followed John to Moline. They settled into a spacious home, large enough to handle a family of eight, with five daughters and one son.

All did not go smoothly for John in Moline. Although the Mississippi offered a route for the quick delivery of quality steel (it now came from Pittsburg rather than England), other problems persisted. Funds were scarce. The farmers buying plows on credit found themselves short on money when a planned crop did not come in.

To increase sales, John set up a large sales operation, and he advertised in newspapers and county fairs. These were new business techniques for companies selling farm tools. Farmers in the surrounding midwestern states, such as Wisconsin and Iowa, could now buy plows from Deere, Tate & Gould through local stores and country peddlers.

John wanted the best possible agents selling for him around the country, so he actively recruited them. To reach farmers in Iowa, John sent one of his new partners, John Gould, to talk to members of the Iowa legislature. From them Gould found out the names and addresses of prominent citizens around the state. Letters soon went out to these people from the Deere, Tate & Gould Company inviting these citizens to join the company's sales force. New salesmen quickly signed up.

Although the Mississippi provided an inexpensive means of getting the plows to towns along the waterway, there was still the problem of getting the plows to inland farmers. Midwestern roads were rough, and railroads traveled only to towns that were on routes to important cities. So the company's agents picked up the plows at shipment points along the river and delivered them directly to the farmers. John emphasized to all his salesmen that their job did not end with the delivery of the plows. The agents had to check back with their customers and keep them satisfied. If improvements could be made to the company's plows, John felt they *should* be made.

John's partners did not always agree. Changes cost extra money. The partners argued that the farmers would just have to take whatever tools the company produced. John disagreed. "If we don't improve our products," he argued, "somebody else will, and we'll lose our trade."

This attitude also made John experiment with products like the grain drill, which planted seeds, and the steam plow. These products eventually developed into important tools for farmers, and Deere was called one of the "pioneers before their time."

On occasion John's urge to improve his tools and make new ones got him into legal trouble. His business practices were often challenged. Serious court squabbles arose about copyrights. Other tool manufacturers claimed that John borrowed ideas too freely, using them as his own. Partners complained that he was too bossy, too headstrong. He made the company change designs too often.

But it was John's belief that he must improve his products in every way possible. John insisted on the highest standards of quality and innovation. "I will never put my name on an implement that does not have the best that is in me."

6

Harvesttime

By the mid-1850s, production had more than tripled at the plow factory. Deere, Tate & Gould were producing over four thousand plows yearly. John wanted his workers to feel a part of the company and to know that their hard work and attention to quality were important contributions. John opened a company boarding house to help his employees save money so they could someday own homes. His workers paid $1.50 a week as rent.

In 1854, sixteen-year-old Charles Deere joined his father's company. The two men worked well together. Young Charles learned the business quickly, rising from a bookkeeper to head salesman and then into an executive role. While John kept his eye on the quality of every company product, Charles watched how every penny was spent.

Charles wrote in a record book, "I will never from this seventh day of February, eighteen hundred sixty A.D. put my name to a paper that I do not expect to pay—so help me God." With such careful financial supervision, John Deere's company truly began to prosper.

In the early 1860s, many southern states withdrew from the United States, and the Civil War began. Illinois was one of the border states between the North and South. Although Illinois remained in the Union, many people in the state supported the Confederacy. John did not. The Moline newspaper mocked John, putting down his arguments against slavery and his fiery defense of all people's right to be free. The *Argus* called him "a raging abolitionist." Still, John did not back down. He stood by his principles.

By the late sixties, after the war had ended, railroads crisscrossed the eastern half of the United States, and bridges spanned the Mississippi. Telegraph wires linked the East Coast to the West Coast, allowing messages to be sent quickly. Improved transportation and communication brought new growth to the Deere company. The list of products expanded. The company now made walking and wheeled plows and cultivators, harrows, drills, planters, wagons, and buggies. Later they even added riding plows and bicycles. Wherever there was a need for a new farming tool, the Deere company tried to fill it.

As the company prospered, so did John. On a bluff overlooking the city, John built a grand family home. From its windows, he could watch the smoke of his company's chimneys, its buildings ever multiplying.

In 1865 Demarius Deere died. John returned to Vermont for the comfort of the family and friends from his youth. He visited Captain Lawrence's daughter Melissa. Demarius's sister, Lucenia Lamb, was also still living in Vermont. John and Lucenia became reacquainted, and eventually John married Lucenia and brought her back to Moline.

In 1868 old partnerships were dissolved, and John Deere's business was officially incorporated under the name Deere & Company. John became the president and Charles the vice president.

As time went on, Charles became the organization's leader, and John's sons-in-law took on important management positions. John no longer spent much time at the company. Instead he joined the ranks of those he had worked so hard to help. He became a farmer.

60

On a large tract of land east of Moline, John raised Jersey cattle and Berkshire hogs. Changing from the finery of earlier years, John now enjoyed roaming his farm in worn clothes, his silver hair glistening in the afternoon sun. The years of working at the forge had hardened his muscles, and his tanned skin stretched smooth and firm.

Deere & Company gradually slipped more and more into the hands of John's children and their spouses. That was fine with John. He had other things to do. Now a wealthy man, he helped to build libraries, orphanages, and churches in Moline and other cities. For a time, he even served as mayor of Moline. As with his business in the past, John's community service involved him in heated arguments and tense situations. But John had learned not to run from trouble.

As John grew older, age began to take a toll on him. It was more and more difficult for him to work his land. But he never lost his interest in his company or his farm. He would have someone drive him out to his properties to check them over.

On the evening of May 17, 1886, at the age of eighty-two, John Deere died in his sleep. At his funeral, flowers banked high around the plain casket he had requested. Nearby stood a plow made of flowers with the inscription *John Deere* on its shaft. Deere's funeral was the biggest Moline had ever witnessed. At the gravesite, three thousand people paid their last respects.

Little did the blacksmith from Vermont realize that when he created his plow to carve a place in the soil, he had also carved himself a place in American history. One of the three plows John made in 1838 now stands displayed in the Smithsonian Institution, in Washington, D. C.

Deere & Company has grown to be the leading manufacturer of farm machinery in the world. On each product manufactured, the name "John Deere" stands out boldly as a credit to the company's creative founder.

Sources

Aldrich, Darragh, *The Story of John Deere.* Minneapolis, Minnesota: privately printed by Charles C. Webber (grandson of John Deere), 1942.

Anderson, Frederick, ed., *Quad Cities: Joined by a River.* Davenport, Iowa: Lee Enterprises, 1982.

Broehl, Wayne G. *John Deere's Company.* New York: Doubleday and Company, 1984.

Clark, Neil M. *John Deere.* Moline, Illinois: DeSaulniers and Company, 1937.

Pierce, Bess, ed., *Moline—A Pictorial History.* Virginia Beach, Virginia: Donning Company, 1981.

Additional acknowledgement is given to the helpful staffs at the Deere & Company Archives Division and the Moline Daily Dispatch.